Jaguars

Victoria Blakemore

For Grandma, with love

© 2018 Victoria Blakemore

Table of Contents

What are Jaguars?   2

Size   4

Physical Characteristics   6

Habitat   8

Range   10

Diet   12

Communication   16

Movement   18

Jaguar Cubs   20

Jaguar Life   22

Black Jaguars   24

Population   26

Jaguars in Danger   28

Helping Jaguars   30

Glossary   34

What Are Jaguars?

Jaguars are large mammals. They are members of the cat family. They are the third largest kind of cat. Only lions and tigers are larger.

Jaguars and leopards look very similar to each other. However, only jaguars have spots inside of the **rosettes** on their fur.

They are usually yellow, orange,

and tan with a white belly and

dark spots. They can also be dark

brown or black.

Size

Jaguars are the largest cat in the Americas. When fully grown, they can be up to six feet long.

Adult jaguars **vary** in weight. They can weigh between 70 and 250 pounds. Jaguars in parts of South America tend to be larger than in other places.

Male jaguars are usually larger

than female jaguars.

Physical Characteristics

Jaguars have very strong legs and large paws. This allows them to be very good climbers.

They have very long whiskers. Their whiskers can help them to sense things that are around them, especially at night when it is very dark.

A jaguar's spots work as **camouflage** to help it sneak up on prey. The spots are like fingerprints, each jaguar has its own pattern.

Habitat

Jaguars are usually found in rainforests, swamps, and grasslands. They prefer areas with lots of plants that help to hide them as they sneak up on prey.

The **climate** is very warm and wet where jaguars live.

Range

Jaguars mainly live in Central and South America. They have also been seen in parts of North America.

They are often found in Brazil, Argentina, Peru, and Mexico. They can also be found in parts of the United States.

Diet

Jaguars are **carnivores**, which means that they eat only meat.

They have been known to eat many different animals. Their diet is usually made up of deer, crocodiles, snakes, sloths, frogs, and fish.

Jaguars have a good sense of smell. They often use it to find their prey.

Jaguars hunt alone. Their sharp claws and strong jaw help them to catch and eat their prey.

They have been known to move their long tail back and forth over the water to attract fish that they can catch and eat.

Jaguars often hide in trees and wait for prey to come by. They jump down to catch it.

Communication

Jaguars use mainly sound and scent to communicate with each other. They can make sounds such as roars, grunts, and meows.

Jaguars mark their **territory** by scraping trees and through their **waste**. It lets other jaguars know that the area is taken.

Like some other big cats, jaguars can roar. They use their roar to defend their **territory** and scare off other animals.

Movement

Jaguars have very strong legs that allow them to be fast runners. They have been known to run up to fifty miles per hour for short distances.

Their strength makes them very good at jumping large distances. They can jump up to nineteen feet in one jump.

Unlike many other big cats, jaguars like the water and often swim or play in rivers.

Jaguar Cubs

Jaguars usually have one or two babies, which are called cubs or kittens. They are born with their eyes closed. Their eyes open after about two weeks.

Cubs stay with their mother for about two years. Then, they leave to find their own **territory**.

Jaguar mothers protect their cubs from predators and teach them how to hunt.

Jaguar Life

Jaguars are **solitary** animals.
They spend most of their time
alone.

Jaguars are usually **nocturnal**.
They are most active and do
their hunting at night. They
often rest when the day is
hottest. They may rest in the
trees or in a den.

Jaguars make their dens in caves or canyons. Some have been found in the ruins of old buildings.

Black Jaguars

Some jaguars have black or dark brown fur. Although they look very different from other jaguars, they are still the same **species**.

These jaguars are **melanistic**. Their skin and fur developed with a dark **pigment**.

Black jaguars may look solid black from far away. If you look closely, you can see that they have darker spots like other jaguars.

Jaguars are not **endangered** yet, but there are not many left in the wild. There are thought to be fewer than 15,000 jaguars left in the wild.

Populations are **declining**. If it continues, they could soon become **endangered.**

In the wild, jaguars often live

between twelve and fifteen years.

They may live longer in **captivity**.

Jaguars in Danger

Jaguars have been hunted for their fur for many years. Their coats are used to make clothing. It is **illegal** to sell jaguar fur, but it still happens.

Jaguars sometimes hunt **livestock** when prey isn't available. They are sometimes hunted to prevent this.

Jaguar habitats are being

destroyed to make space for

mining, farming, or logging.

Helping Jaguars

There are several ways that people are trying to help jaguars. Researchers track wild jaguars to learn more about them and where they live.

In some places, areas of rainforest are protected. This provides animals such as jaguars a safe habitat.

In some places, jaguars that are born in **captivity** are trained to survive in the wild. When they are old enough, they are released.

Other groups focus on education. They want people to learn as much as they can about jaguars so they can help them.

Glossary

Camouflage: using color to blend in to the surroundings

Captivity: animals that are kept by humans, not in the wild

Carnivore: an animal that eats only meat

Climate: the usual weather in a place

Declining: getting smaller

Endangered: at risk of becoming extinct

Illegal: against the law

Melanistic: when an animal's genes cause it to have darker skin or fur than is normal

Nocturnal: animals that are most active at night

Pigment: the natural color of a part of a plant or animal

Rosettes: circular markings

Solitary: living alone

Species: a group of the same kind of living things

Territory: an area of land that an animal clams as its own

Vary: differ

Waste: material given off by the body after food is digested

About the Author

Victoria Blakemore is a first grade

teacher in Southwest Florida with a

passion for reading.

You can visit her at

www.elementaryexplorers.com

Also in This Series

Gray Wolves
Sloths
Flamingos
Camels
Koalas
Honey Bees
Pandas

Pangolins
White-Tailed Deer
Orcas
Giraffes
Corn
Meerkats
Echidnas

Walruses
Raccoons
Bald Eagles
Apples
Arctic Foxes
Red Pandas
Cassowaries

Tigers
Ladybugs
Moose
Beluga Whales
Leopards
Elephants
Jellyfish

Binturongs
Lions
Dolphins
Reindeer
Hammerhead Sharks
Hippos
Pumpkins

Peafowl
Chameleons
Florida Panthers
Aye-Ayes
Black Bears
Cheetahs
Manatees

Gingerbread
Polar Bears
Hot Chocolate
Orangutans
Coyotes
Marshmallows
Strawberries

Also in This Series

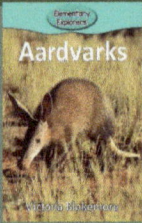

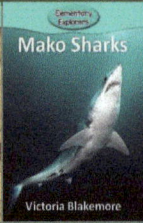

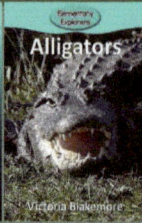

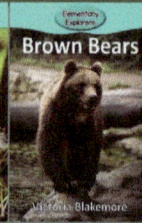

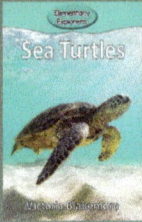

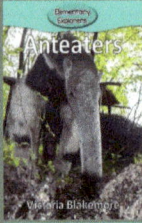

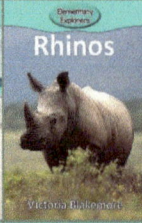

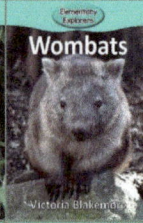

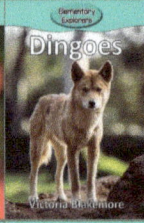

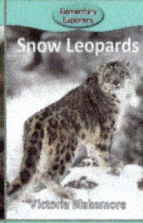

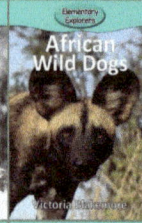

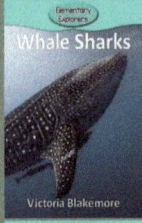

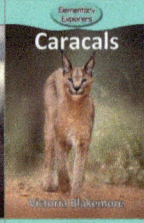

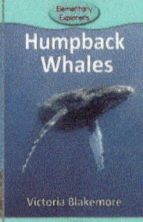

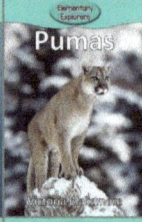

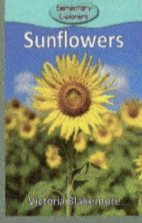

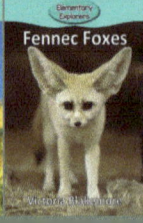

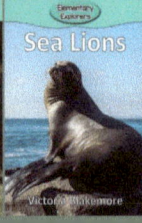

Aardvarks	Mako Sharks	Alligators	Frogs	Hedgehogs	Brown Bears	Bongos
Sea Turtles	Quokkas	Muskrats	Zebras	Red Foxes	Ring-Tailed Lemurs	Platypuses
Anteaters	Kangaroos	Rhinos	Jaguars	Wombats	Capybaras	Gorillas
Cats	Skunks	Butterflies	Dingoes	Snow Leopards	African Wild Dogs	Penguins
Whale Sharks	Wolverines	Warthogs	Caracals	Badgers	Seals	Hummingbirds
Pikas	Humpback Whales	Pumas	Lemonade	Llamas	Tulips	Ostriches
Sunflowers	Fennec Foxes	Sea Lions	Squirrels	Roses	Porcupines	Ice Cream

All titles: Elementary Explorers — Victoria Blakemore

www.ingramcontent.com/pod-product-compliance
Lightning Source LLC
Chambersburg PA
CBHW051252020426
42333CB00025B/3171